I0409163

Buddhist Wisdom for Business Success

Table of Contents

Chapter 1. Introduction

Unearth the profound synergy of ancient philosophy and modern business strategy with our special report, "Buddhist Wisdom for Business Success." Dive deep into a transformational journey that harmonizes age-old Buddhist principles with present-day corporate necessities. This enlightening exploration will provide you with unconventional yet efficacious tools, directly sourced from the wisdom of the Buddha, that promise to stimulate growth, foster creative solutions and encourage a harmonious, resilient business environment. This isn't your usual business playbook, but an invitation to an enthralling trek into a blend of wisdom and pragmatism that has proven to be a game-changer in the sphere of business. Prepare to ascend to unprecedented heights of success with our unorthodox, yet compelling approach. Let's trailblaze together! Venture forth and grab your copy now - brace yourself for a revolution in your business prowess!

Chapter 2. Unveiling Buddhist Wisdom: An Unorthodox Guide to Business Success

The ties that bind the teachings of Buddhism and the modern business scene may seem unexpected to many. After all, they seemingly exist in disparate dimensions, one being thousands of years old with spiritual origins, and the other being a relatively modern construct grounded in a drive for material growth and achievement. Yet the principles embedded within Buddhism's rich and profound heritage have far-reaching implications which can transform and truly thrive within a corporate setting.

2.1. The Four Noble Truths: Pivoting Ideas into Action

Parallels between the Four Noble Truths and the process of bringing a business idea into a fruitful venture are undeniable. At the core of these four pillars of Buddhism lie hard truths about existence, suffering and the path toward liberation - truths that aren't very different when it comes to launching and growing a business.

The first truth is the acknowledgment of the existence of suffering, in business, this translates to acknowledging that difficulties, obstacles, and solutions are a part of the journey. A new venture always comes with challenges. Just like in life, it's not these challenges that define us, but how we respond to them. This is the second truth, understanding the cause of suffering. In the business context, it's the identification of these obstacles and challenges.

The third truth is essentially the cessation to suffering. In businesses, this could signify brainstorming solutions and executing strategies to overcome the challenges. The final and fourth noble truth is the path that leads to the cessation of suffering or reaching a desired level of success in business through determination, strategy, and action.

2.2. The Middle Path: Balancing Profit and Purpose

In Buddhism, the Middle Path is a practical approach to avoid both indulgence and deprivation. Translated in business, this balance manifests as finding the equilibrium between profit and purpose. Of course, profits are necessary for a business to survive and grow, but a purpose-driven approach is what differentiates great companies from good ones.

To adopt the Middle Path in your business, your primary aim should be to balance two main components: financial returns and value creation for your stakeholders (customers, employees, community). This may involve making strategic decisions geared toward sustainable, long-term growth over short-term wins

2.3. The Three Marks of Existence: Change, Selflessness, and Nirvana

The three marks of existence offer another essential lesson for the business world. Impermanence (anicca), non-self (anatta), and nirvana are the concepts that signify change, selflessness, and peace, respectively.

Understanding impermanence or Anicca, businesses can embrace change instead of running from it. Just as nothing is permanent in life, market trends, customer needs, and industry specifications will never stay the same in the business. Becoming adaptable to this constant change can put you on the fast track to success.

The concept of non-self, Anatta, implies the absence of an unchanging, permanent self. This can inspire organizational leaders to encourage collaborative effort rather than fostering an individualistic approach within their teams.

Finally, Nirvana. Bringing this concept into businesses means aiming for a state of ultimate satisfaction and peace. Upper echelons or managers can cultivate this by encouraging work-life balance, fostering a sense of contentment, and promoting mindfulness.

2.4. Applying Buddhist Ethics: Right Intention, Right Action

The main ethical conduct laid down by Buddha are the concepts of Right Intention and Right Action, elements of the Eightfold Path. In the current business world saturated with companies getting embroiled in scandals and frauds, these are ethics that can be the bedrock of a firm's principles and policies.

Right Intention infers that actions should stem from feelings of goodwill, non-hatred, and non-violence. This can materialize as an organization's intention to do good for the community, stakeholders, and the environment.

Right Action refers to actions that are honest, decent, and morally acceptable. Companies can implement this by discarding any corrupt practices and ensuring fair dealings with all involved parties.

Encoding these principles into your business strategy is not a one-day affair; it's a road of resilience and unending learning. But as you incorporate and align yourself with these timeless principles, you'll start seeing the transformation. Not only in your growth metrics but in the overall harmony, resilience, and creativity your venture begins to exhibit. This is the essence of Buddhist wisdom for business success - an unorthodox, yet practical toolbox for the modern-day corporates. So, continue to challenge the norm, take the road less traveled, and ignite your journey to sustainable prosperity.

Chapter 3. Mindfulness in Management: Leading with Awareness and Compassion

In the hustle and bustle of the corporate world, where the stakes are high and pressures immense, a manager's best tool can often be forged from hundreds of miles and many centuries away - from the concepts of mindfulness and compassion, pillars of Buddhist philosophy. By cultivating and harnessing these qualities within the context of management, businesses can cultivate strong, resilient, and forward-thinking leaders...

3.1. The Philosophy of Mindfulness

Simply put, mindfulness is the practice of bringing full, nonjudgmental awareness to our present moment's experience. Unlike being lost in thoughts about the past or future, mindfulness explores the present in a clear, calm, and collected way.

In the business world, it could translate to paying undivided attention during a meeting, actively listening to an employee's contributions, or fully focusing on a task at hand. When leaders embrace mindfulness, they can make more informed decisions as they can observe and assimilate information impartially, potentially leading to better outcomes.

3.2. Cultivating Mindfulness in the Corporate Environment

The first step in incorporating mindfulness in the corporate setting is understanding that it's not just a leadership tool; it's a culture. It must permeate all interactions and processes within an organization. Here are a few practical ways to nurture mindfulness:

- Start meetings with a moment of silence. This allows everyone to get centered and present, creating a more productive conversation.

- Encourage regular breaks. Short rests in between tasks keep stress at bay and enhance focus.

- Offer mindfulness training or workshops. It will provide employees with tools to reduce stress, increase productivity, and improve overall well-being.

3.3. Compassion in Leadership

Compassion is the wish to alleviate suffering. In the context of business management, it means understanding the struggles of your team, offering help, and fostering a supportive team spirit. It is about creating an environment that underscores empathy, respect, and kindness - qualities that inspire loyalty and foster improved productivity among employees.

3.4. Compassion: The Catalyst for Resilient Business Relationships

Building compassion isn't about being overly sentimental or shying away from difficult conversations. It's about recognizing that every member of the team has something valuable to contribute and needs to be treated as an essential part of the collective success.

Developing compassion as a leader could involve understanding your team's strengths and weaknesses, genuinely listening to their feedback, and assisting them when needed. A compassionate leader fosters an open, inclusive environment where every voice matters, and all ideas are appreciated.

3.5. The Intersection of Mindfulness and Compassion in Management

When mindfulness and compassion are woven into the fabric of management, a profound transformation begins to unfold within an organization. Decision-making becomes clearer, more inclusive, and better aligned with the actual needs of the business and the people who make it function every day. Our interactions are also more genuine and honest. We become more adept at finding joy in the success of our peers, and we become more resilient to inevitable setbacks.

By fostering an environment that champions mindfulness and compassion, businesses, large and small, can cultivate a new breed of leaders – leaders who understand that success isn't just about the bottom line. And that success is ultimately about growing together as a team and fostering a workplace that values the well-being and input of all its members – with kindness, respect, and understanding at its core.

To navigate the complex world of business management with grace, awareness, and effectiveness, we must turn to mindfulness and compassion. As we draw lessons from Buddhist teachings, we realize that the most successful businesses are not just the ones that generate profits, but those that nurture the growth of their people and contribute positively to society. Embrace this philosophy, and you'll not only be a successful manager but a transformational leader.

The harmony of mindfulness and compassion in management will definitely be a revolution in business operations and interpersonal dynamics. As leaders, it's time we route our management skills into a more comprehensive, effective, and compassionate direction. It is inevitable that trials and challenges will occur, but a mindful and compassionate resolution always carries the solution.

As leaders, creating a culture of mindfulness and compassion is the first step towards an engaged, happy, and effective workforce. Lead with compassion. Manage with mindfulness. This is the path to lasting success in the inherently unpredictable world of business.

Chapter 4. The Eightfold Path: A Revolutionary Business Strategy

As we set forth on an unprecedented journey of corporate enlightenment, it is integral to recognize the Eightfold Path as outlined by the Buddha and its profound implications on modern-day business. Transforming these principles into a business strategy might initially seem far-fetched, yet with careful observation, it unfolds with great relevance and poetic synchronicity.

4.1. Understanding Reality

Every sound strategy starts with understanding - deeply grasping the nature of things. In the business landscape, this translates to understanding market dynamics, customer behaviors, competitors' strategies, societal influencing factors, and of course, your own strengths and weaknesses. The deeper your understanding of these elements, the more effective your strategy will be.

Take, for example, Netflix's groundbreaking transition from DVD-rental to streaming that fully leveraged their understanding of changing customer preferences and technological advancements. Here lies the essence of Right Understanding or **Samma Ditthi** in the context of business - recognizing the changing nature of market dynamics and responding accordingly.

4.2. Thoughtful Decision Making

Right Intention, or **Samma Sankappa**, emphasizes the importance of purpose, commitment, and reason in your undertakings. As Business leaders, every decision must be reasoned, in line with the company's mission and values, and made with genuine commitment. Only then can they withstand turbulent times or sharp scrutiny.

Microsoft's environmental pledge exemplifies this. By 2030, they aim to be carbon negative, and by 2050, they aspire to remove from the environment all the carbon they have emitted since their establishment in 1975. This level of commitment and cognizant decision-making displays the essence of the second element of the Eightfold Path vividly.

4.3. Effective Communication

To create a thriving business ecosystem, the importance of Right Speech, or **Samma Vaca**, cannot be understated. Effective, honest, and clear communication amongst stakeholders promotes transparency and trust, leading to healthier collaborations and partnerships.

Tesla CEO, Elon Musk, known for his relentless authenticity, underscores the importance of honest communication in both internal affairs and public relations. He also shines light on the potential harm brought by malicious speech, through his own experiences being sued for defamation over a single tweet.

4.4. Ethical Business Conduct

Right Action, **Samma Kammanta**, involves acting in ways that are morally and ethically sound. In business, this could mean ensuring fair trade, respecting labor rights, environmental responsibility, and abiding by honesty in every transaction.

The unmistakable case of the Volkswagen emission crisis shows us that unethical actions might provide short-term benefits, but they eventually lead to legal issues, reputational damage, and enormous fines.

4.5. Ethical Livelihood

Right Livelihood, or **Samma Ajiva**, asserts the importance of making a living through ethical and fair means. In business, it showcases the vitality of the nature of your products, services, and operations that don't harm or deceive others. Take the example of companies like Patagonia, that prioritize ethical sourcing and sustainable practices.

4.6. Consistent Effort

In business, consistency is key. Right Effort, or **Samma Vayama**, elucidates the vitality of perseverance and constant attempt to improve irrespective of challenges. It involves refining one's strategies and learning from mistakes to eventually succeed, as demonstrated by companies like Airbnb and Slack, which started in completely different industries but hit their stride after strategic pivots.

4.7. Mindfulness and Awareness

Right Mindfulness, or **Samma Sati**, refers to being mentally alert, aware, and engrossed in thoughts and actions. In business, this can reflect the practice of conscious leadership. Leaders who practice awareness not only promote a pleasant work environment, but also inspire their followers to be mindful in their roles. Google's "Search Inside Yourself" program, aimed to train employees in mindfulness, is a shining example.

4.8. Focused Approach

Finally, Right Concentration, or **Samma Samadhi**, means channeling focus on your objectives without being overwhelmed by distractions. In business, a successful example could be Apple, focusing on a few products but doing them impeccably.

In conclusion, the Buddha's Eightfold Path provides an unconventional viewpoint on strategizing business activities. Its focus on understanding, intention, communication, action, livelihood, effort, mindfulness, and concentration uncannily aligns with the pillars required to build a thriving, resilient, and successful enterprise. Subtly ingrained in the businesses of today, this wisdom can revolutionize the way industries operate and leaders lead. The unprecedented fusion of Buddhist philosophy and business strategy can, thus, serve as a beacon of enlightened performance in the corporate world.

Chapter 5. Creating a Company Culture of Balance & Harmony

In Buddhist philosophy, balance and harmony are more than ideals; they represent the enlightened state of being, synonymous with inner peace, content happiness, and attaining Nirvana. Similarly, in the corporate world, a balanced and harmonious company culture bears the fruit of prosperity, innovation, and a sustainable competitive edge. In this chapter, we will delve into creating a harmonious, well-balanced corporate culture, utilizing timeless Buddhist teachings as our guiding principles.

5.1. The Pillars of Balance

Balance, in Buddhism, is the middle way, the ideal moderation between extremes. It reflects having the wisdom to avoid overindulgence and deprivation. Drawing parallels to the business realm, this means creating a workspace where hard work and relaxation, individuality and teamwork, stability and innovation co-exist - a balanced corporate culture.

The essence of a balanced workplace is in providing employees the freedom to innovate while having a structure to guide them, encouraging teamwork while promoting individual growth, and expecting continued high performance while advocating for leisure. Balance is multifaceted and reflects in several aspects of corporate culture:

1. Balance in Decision-making: Promote both data-driven and intuitive decision-making practices. Each has its place. Data ensures decisions are grounded in facts, while intuition allows for the exploration of uncharted territory.

2. Balance in Leadership: Leadership style needs a blend of transactional and transformational approaches. While the transactional approach facilitates the daily workflow, transformational leadership fuels growth and innovation.

3. Balance in Workload: Ensure workloads are challenging but not overwhelming. This helps avoid burnout and fosters a sense of achievement.

5.2. Creating a Harmonious Environment

In Buddhist belief, harmony is not mere agreement but a state where differences coexist peacefully. In business terms, harmony in the workplace represents the congenial existence of diverse employees working collectively towards common business goals. Achieving this requires attention to factors like communication, mutual respect, and shared vision.

1. Open and Clear Communication: Foster a culture of open dialogue where employees are free to express their views, ideas, and difficulties without fear. Clear communication reduces misunderstanding, enables faster problem-solving, and promotes a sense of involvement.

2. Mutual Respect: Encourage respect for every individual, irrespective of their role, gender, age, or ethnic background. Understanding and acceptance of differences breed mutual respect and a more inclusive work culture.

3. Shared Vision: Everyone in the company should understand and align with the organization's goals and values. A shared long-term mission works like a compass guiding everyone towards collective success.

5.3. Building a Mindful Workforce

Mindfulness, the practice of being fully present and engaged in one's current activity, is central to Buddhist philosophy and can be a powerful tool for creating a harmonious, productive work environment. Mindfulness strengthens focus, boosts creativity, reduces stress, and fosters empathy – all crucial for a balanced and harmonious company culture.

Employers can nurture mindfulness in the workplace in several ways:

1. Mindful Meetings: Start meetings with a 'mindful minute' where everyone is asked to focus on their breath. This centers the group and clears the clutter of distractions, promoting more effective communication.

2. Offering Mindfulness Training: Workshops or courses about mindfulness help develop a deep understanding and encourages integration into daily work-life.

3. Encouraging Mindful Breaks: Promote the habit of taking short, mindful breaks where employees relax and re-energize. This can significantly enhance productivity and creativity.

5.4. Walking the Middle Path: Putting Principles Into Practice

Companies looking to create a balanced and harmonious corporate culture should embrace the Buddha's Eightfold Path. This comprises right understanding, right thought, right speech, right action, right livelihood, right effort, right mindfulness, and right concentration. Much like the interlocking pieces of a jigsaw puzzle, the pieces of this path form a comprehensive model for ethical, mindful, and balanced corporate governance.

1. Right Understanding and Right Thought: Promote knowledge sharing and continuous learning. Encourage ethical decision making and foster a culture of creative, problem-solving mentality.

2. Right Speech, Right Action, and Right Livelihood: Communicate honestly, act transparently, and uphold corporate social responsibility.

3. Right Effort, Right Mindfulness, and Right Concentration: Encourage a blend of efficiency and effort, promote mindfulness, and support focused work.

Creating a corporate culture that exudes balance and harmony is indeed a journey more than a destination. Companies that succeed in blending the wisdom of Buddhism with modern corporate strategy are likely to see not only increased productivity and innovation but also a happier, more motivated workforce – a sure recipe for sustained success in the ever-changing business environment.

Let us dare to tread this unconventional path that harmoniously integrates ancient wisdom and pragmatic business strategies. Let's embrace balance, foster harmony, and create a resilient business environment. After all, in the wise words of Buddha, "Just as a candle cannot burn without fire, men cannot live without a spiritual life." An enlightened company culture is the flame that drives the corporate world, illuminates our path to success, and enkindles growth and prosperity. Let's kindle that flame and illuminate our path towards a harmonious corporate culture that synergizes timeless wisdom and modern strategies for unparalleled success.

Chapter 6. Impermanence: Embracing Change in a Volatile Market

Markets, by their very nature, are volatile. They are in a constant state of flux, driven by economic cycles, political happenings, technological advancements, and social moods. This volatility is often perceived negatively, an impetus for uncertainty, and fear. However, in the heart of Buddhist philosophy, we find a different perspective, centered on the acceptance of change and the impermanence of all things. This philosophy can guide us to thrive amidst uncertainty, just as a lotus thrives in a muddy pond.

6.1. Transforming the Perception of Change

The Buddhist principle of impermanence – or 'anicca' in Pali – comes from an understanding that everything we experience through our senses, everything we might think or imagine, are all characterized by the three marks of existence: unsatisfactoriness, not-self, and most importantly for our purposes, impermanence. So, if change and variability are essentially inherent in all of existence, why not embrace it as a natural aspect of markets and as an opportunity for growth and progress?

To thrive in this volatile landscape, we must first transform our perception of change. Rather than resisting volatility, fearing it, or running from it, why not strive to understand it? We should foster a mindset of exploring the unknown territories of change, adapting our strategies accordingly. By doing so, we courageously confront change, anticipating and embracing its spontaneous nature. This paradigm shift fosters a more agile, resilient, and ultimately successful business environment.

6.2. Cultivating Mindfulness: The Key to Navigating Change

If change is the only constant, then how do we navigate it? The Buddha's teachings provide us with an essential tool: mindfulness. Being mindful means being fully present, anchored in the current moment, receiving and observing things just as they are without judgement. It fosters an acute awareness of the inner and outer transformations in ourselves, our organization, and our marketplace, without getting trapped in a constant desire for stability.

In the realm of business, mindfulness can be a powerful ally. By cultivating mindfulness within our teams and within ourselves, we can better recognize changes in consumer demands, marketplace trends, and even subtle transformations within our own organizations. We are then better equipped to respond to these changes in an informed and timely manner.

6.3. An Impermanent Business Model is a Resilient Business Model

Given that the only thing permanent is impermanence itself, our business models should reflect this truth. By creating flexible, adaptable business models, we avoid the pitfalls of rigidity in the face of market fluctuations.

Today's advancements in technology have led to disruptions in various business landscapes, often leaving companies that fail to adapt behind. Understanding that change is inevitable allows us to take a proactive stance by consistently re-evaluating and updating our offerings, production methods, and business models. This does not only keep us relevant, but it also allows us to lead change and drive innovation.

6.4. Weathering the Storm - Building Resilience

Blockbuster, Kodak, and Nokia - these are just a few examples of once-thriving businesses rendered obsolete due to their failure to adapt to marketplace changes. They serve as solemn reminders of the significance of agility and flexibility in our volatile business platform.

Building resilience in your organization requires instilling a culture that not only tolerifies change but sees it as invigorating rather than threatening. Such a culture encourages innovation, creative problem-solving and adaptability, essential components for survival in any business ecosystem. Mindfulness goes hand in hand in achieving this as it fosters acceptance of the present moment and facilitates change.

6.5. Impermanence as a Healing, Unifying Force

Fostering a view of change as a natural process can create a more harmonious work environment. As members of a team become adept at navigating changes together, tensions caused by unpredictability can decrease. This collective journey through the tumultuous waves of change can also serve as a unifying force, tightening the bonds between team members.

Impermanence is not about fearing change, but embracing its transformative potential. Change is an inevitable part of our existence. So why not take a leaf out of the Buddha's teachings and use this understanding to inspire foresight, cultivate resilience, and nurture a healthier, adaptable business ecosystem?

By starkly recognizing the impermanence that underlies the volatile market, we see that we bear an immense capacity to not just weather the storm but navigate it with precision and confidence. Embracing change, we then create a more harmonious, innovative, and ultimately successful enterprise. Yes, change can often breed uncertainty, yet with the right perspective, it can also breed untamed possibilities for innovation, growth, and ultimate success.

Chapter 7. Four Noble Truths for Business Problem-Solving & Innovation

We often think of problem-solving and innovation as modern constructs, but in fact, their roots are deeply embedded in age-old philosophies, such as Buddhism. The Four Noble Truths, first put forth by Buddha over 2,500 years ago, is not just a spiritual directive but constitutes a remarkably fitting framework for contemporary business challenges.

7.1. Recognizing the Problem: Dukkha

The First Noble Truth of Buddhism, Dukkha, often translates to suffering or dissatisfaction. In business, this is akin to identifying that a problem or stagnancy exists. Is the company experiencing lowered sales, low employee morale, rising costs or any other discomfort? Dig deep, survey the terrain, and uncover the reality of your situation. Translating Dukkha to the business paradigm compels us to acknowledge business realities, however unpleasant they may be.

To genuinely capture the essence of Dukkha in your enterprise, focus on visibility and openness. Listen actively to managers, teams, and front-line employees. Look beyond the apparent and delve into the root of the issue. Use a blend of quantitative data and qualitative insights. Tools like SWOT analysis, PESTLE, Porter's Five Forces, employee surveys, and customer feedback could be invaluable here.

7.2. Understanding the Cause: Samudaya

Having identified the business problem (Dukkha), we must then comprehend its origins or causative factors. This is the core notion behind the Second Noble Truth: Samudaya. Buddha believed suffering is born out of desire or attachment, which provides an apt metaphor for businesses. Many problems arise from inexorable adherence to old strategies, fear of change, or greed for short-term gains.

Investigate the patterns, trace the correlations, and derive causative factors from your assembled data and feedback. Ask 'why' multiple times until you uncover the real cause rather than surface-level symptoms. Agile practices like A3 problem-solving, Fishbone Diagram, or Five Whys Technique are useful here. Also, adopt a customer-centric lens to ensure you're not falling prey to being overly attached to your perspectives, losing sight of market realities.

7.3. Envisioning the Solution: Nirodha

The Third Noble Truth of Buddhism is 'Nirodha' - the cessation of suffering. The compelling vision of a problem-free state can provide a powerful motivator for change.

Begin by defining what success would look like within the context of your problem. Is it increased employee morale? A reduction in costs? An improved market share? Quantify these goals where possible to make them measurable. Work with teams across the organisation, using tools like 'OGSM' (Objectives, Goals, Strategies, Measures) to drill down to action plans. The envisioning process is pivotal since it sets the direction for all subsequent strategic choices.

7.4. The Path to Resolution: Magga

Finally, Magga - the Fourth Noble Truth - is the path leading to the cessation of suffering. In the business context, it's the solution or set of strategies your organization needs to employ to resolve the problem and reach your envisioned state.

This path depends on your problem and solution instances, and could involve a plethora of strategic choices. You might need to iterate your offerings, pivot your business model, invest in digital transformation, or conceptualize a new product line based on market trends. Leverage collective intelligence; involve cross-functional teams in defining your 'Middle Way' - a sustainable, balanced path to your goal.

7.5. Innovation Informed by the Four Noble Truths

Innovation resonates with the Four Noble Truths as they share similar attributes. We identify problems or gaps (Dukkha), find their cause or origin (Samudaya), envision a potential solution (Nirodha), and execute that solution (Magga). It is this cycle that allows companies to disrupt and push boundaries.

Buddha's wisdom is not just spiritual, it's timeless and universally applicable, even in corporate boardrooms. When we recognize that dealing with the 'Dukkha' of corporate realities is not separate from life's realities, we're able to apply the Four Noble Truths to strategic thinking and operational execution.

A nuanced understanding of this approach's potency can revolutionize how you perceive business growth. It drives towards an absolute, yet somewhat ignored, truth - that businesses are any society's microcosm. Therefore, they can infer huge benefits from lessons taught by one of the most enlightened minds in history.

Buddha's teachings provide an intensely realistic yet compassionate guide to success, encouraging us to balance ambition with empathy and pragmatism with mindfulness.

In our quest for stability and growth amid chaos and uncertainty, these ancient principles provide a guiding light to navigate with wisdom, compassion, and resilience. By integrating these beliefs into our business strategy, we encourage enterprises not only to succeed but to contribute positively to the world.

Chapter 8. Transpierce Barriers: How to Practice Non-attachment in Business

An essential tenant of Buddhism, non-attachment, is also a potent practice in the realm of business. Non-attachment doesn't imply disinterest or disregard for outcomes. Rather, it encourages a focus on actions and efforts, weight on the present moment, and liberation from the clutches of outcomes that we can't fully control. The practice of non-attachment can help business professionals develop equanimity, resilience, and adaptability, fostering sustainable success.

8.1. The Foundation of Non-Attachment

According to Buddhism, craving or desire is the primary cause of suffering. This craving can emerge in various forms, one of which is attachment. Attachment refers to the binding emotion towards people, possessions, or outcomes. Overwhelming attachment, according to Buddhist wisdom, forms a barrier preventing us from experiencing reality as it truly is, and instead, we remain incarcerated in our subjective perceptions and expectations.

As business leaders, our attachment to the outcome often impedes our discernment. We hold too firmly to a particular vision, become blind to feasible alternatives, uncontrollable influences, or changing market trends. Consequently, we find ourselves trapped in emotional turmoil, reacting inappropriately to challenges and disruptions, and eroding our mental peace and overall efficiency.

Non-attachment, in this regard, allows us a balanced perspective. It encourages us to continue striving for objectives, while acknowledging the nebulous nature of outcomes. In business, non-attachment is less about restricting ambition and more about engaging wholeheartedly in the process, uninhibited by preconceptions of success or failure.

8.2. Non-Attachment: Not Detachment

A common misconception about non-attachment is it's synonymous with detachment. Detachment often suggests escape – pulling away from emotions, involvement, and responsibility. This is not what non-attachment promotes. Non-attachment, instead, encourages participation and engagement without being bound by expectations.

In a business scenario, practicing non-attachment could mean developing a product with passion and commitment, embodying the understanding that its market performance relies on several elements beyond our control. It might mean behaving ethically and responsibly, without letting the competitive market pressure push you into ill-suited decisions, allowing the tranquillity of mind and clarity of actions to guide you through ups and downs.

8.3. Adopting Non-Attachment in Business

The implementation of non-attachment in business isn't a one-step process but a continuum that needs to be integrated into corporate culture and personal ethos.

1. **Focus on Effort, not Outcome:** Buddhist wisdom emphasises the significance of the act, not the result. Exert complete effort into the process and let go of the anxiety associated with the outcome. Allow the fruits of your endeavor to ripen organically.

2. **Practice Mindfulness:** Non-attachment requires immersing oneself attentively in the current moment. Mindfulness fosters an acute awareness of our attachments and provides us the wisdom to navigate them.

3. **Lead with Compassion:** When a business leader exercises compassion, s/he enables a supportive environment that motivates the team to participate enthusiastically, without fear of judgment or failure.

4. **Cultivate Flexibility:** Non-attachment encourages us to be fluid and adaptable, open to exploring varied pathways to an objective, non-resistant to changes or novel opportunities.

5. **Embrace Uncertainty:** It is the only certainty in business. Accept it with a calm mind instead of intolerance or fear, and utilize it as a dynamic force for innovation.

8.4. Resilience: The Byproduct of Non-Attachment

One of the tangible benefits of practicing non-attachment in business is increased resilience. When we are overly attached to a specific outcome, we crumble when things don't go as planned. Subsequently, the recovery becomes arduous.

Non-attachment, however, amplifies our tolerance to setbacks, impediments, and delays. It rolls out a perspective that views failures not as devastating ends but as forks in the journey to success. Resilience, enriched by non-attachment, instills in us an unyielding spirit that relentlessly continues the pursuit of objectives, unaffected by transitory hurdles and unanticipated outcomes.

8.5. The Success of Non-Attachment

In a world where success is often equated to possessions, victories, or accolades, non-attachment introduces an alternative conception of success that isn't confined to physical or measurable accomplishments but inclusive of enduring mind tranquility, unshakeable resolve, steady diligence, and the courage to endure the unpredictability of business with serenity.

In conclusion, the practice of non-attachment in business can stimulate a paradigm shift, magnifying our focus on the journey rather than the destination, fostering flexibility, enhancing resilience, and encouraging genuine joy in our exertions. By embracing non-attachment, we find ourselves not in the inconstant rapture of momentary success, but the constant bliss of unshakeable equanimity, an asset more precious and enduring than any tangible achievement. Undoubtedly, non-attachment can serve as a potent instrument in our arsenal to transpierce the barriers standing between us and the unprecedented growth that awaits us.

Chapter 9. The Circle of Interdependence and Business Sustainability

In observing the observed order of nature, the Buddha discovered what he termed the principle of 'Pratityasamutpada' or 'Dependent Origination.' This elemental teaching reminds us that everything in existence, every phenomenon, depends upon a myriad of conditions for its manifestation - there is no independence, only interdependence.

From the tiny seed that requires fertile soil, nourishing moisture, the right temperature, and countless other factors to become a great tree, to complexes of businesses that hinge on markets, labor, materials, knowledge, technology, and a plethora of other components, everything exists because of everything else.

Recognizing and respecting this interdependence is pivotal, not only to achieving business sustainability but also to unlocking potential for exceptional breakthroughs. By viewing a business as part of an interconnected network - of industries, communities, and natural systems - we can create strategies that align with the principles of harmony, balance, and support for all linkages, leading to sustainable prosperity.

9.1. Embracing the Interconnectedness

Companies operate within larger ecosystems that encompass employees, customers, partners, communities, and the environment. These stakeholders are interconnected and are as much a part of an organization's success as its leadership and products or services.

Understanding how these connections interact and impact one another is crucial to creating a sustainable business model. Similarly, recognizing and accounting for the indirect repercussions of decision-making - what Buddhists refer to as the 'karma' of the organization - ensures a mindful approach that considers the well-being and future health of all stakeholders.

A Buddhist-inspired strategy might include initiatives like prioritizing employee well-being, building fair and symbiotic supply chain partnerships, providing value with integrity to customers, extending support to local communities, and adopting environment-friendly practices that contribute to the planet's health.

9.2. Mindful Decision-Making

Incorporating a mindful lens to business decision-making can lead to sustainable growth and benefits for all stakeholders. This approach involves continually assessing the foreseeable impacts and potential unforeseen consequences of choices before taking action. Essentially, one should strive to minimize harm and promote wellbeing within our sphere of influence.

Consider the decision-making around sourcing materials for production. A mindful choice could mean selecting ethically-sourced raw materials—a decision that may initially seem to increase expenses. However, it can lead to long-term benefits such as building a responsible brand reputation, enabling new partnership opportunities, and motivating employees who prefer working for responsible businesses. The ripple effects of a single mindful decision can therefore positively affect the entire chain of interdependence, reinforcing the principles of sustainable business practices.

9.3. The Middle Way in Business

A fundamental precept in Buddhism is the 'Middle Way' - the path of moderation and balance, avoiding extremes. This principle translates seamlessly to business strategy. Businesses that seek both profit and purpose, balancing the needs of all stakeholders, will find themselves on a sustainable path.

The Middle Way in business implies avoiding an extreme focus on just shareholder profits or purely societal benefits. Like in Buddhism where the Middle Way avoids self-indulgence and self-mortification, businesses should steer clear of overindulging in profit-seeking at the expense of other stakeholders or neglecting their viability by overly focusing on societal issues.

With this balanced approach, businesses can build resilience, foster loyalty among stakeholders, and ensure their sustained relevance in the market.

9.4. Compassion and Business Leadership

Just as interdependence reveals the wisdom of the Middle Way, it also highlights the importance of compassion in business. The Buddha taught that once we see the interconnectedness of all beings, we naturally cultivate kindness towards others, as we understand that their happiness or suffering ultimately affects us too.

Leaders practicing compassion work towards the welfare of all stakeholders, fostering a positive, inclusive, and nurturing work environment that leads to a committed, innovative, and productive workforce. Simultaneously, compassion towards customers leads to services and products that truly meet their needs, creating loyal patronage and long-lasting relationships.

Understanding the Circle of Interdependence reaffirms the criticality of business sustainability, not as a 'nice-to-have' but as an essential strategy for survival, growth, and making a meaningful difference.

As we acknowledge our connections to each other and the planet, we align our strategies with the foundational principles of harmony, mutual support, and long-term prosperity, creating businesses that are resilient, innovative, and enriching for all.

Chapter 10. Meditative Leadership: Cultivating Focus and Clarity

We live in a world defined by speed, efficiency, and ceaseless activity. But what if there was another path to success, one less traveled yet profoundly transformative in its approach? One that derives directly from the wisdom of the great Buddha, harmoniously blending ancient principles with modern necessities - Meditative Leadership.

Leadership is more than just a role or a job title. It is the ability to guide, influence, and inspire. And to do so effectively, it demands a high degree of focus and clarity, two qualities that are regrettably scarce in today's frenzied corporate world. Yet, cultivating these qualities can be achieved, paving the pathway to a more streamlined, effective, and enlightened organization. So, let's begin our journey towards Meditative Leadership.

10.1. The Concept of Meditative Leadership

Meditative Leadership refers to the incorporation of meditative principles and practices into leadership. It's about bringing calmness, clarity, and mindfulness to the forefront of any decision-making process while fostering a more focused workplace environment.

The Buddha taught, "Do not dwell in the past, do not dream of the future, concentrate the mind on the present moment." It's this tenet that Meditative Leadership embraces, keeping leaders grounded in the present moment, detached from external distractions, personal biases, and undercurrents of ego that frequently seep into corporate decision-making.

Meditative Leadership fundamentally alters the way leaders engage with their teams and make decisions. It flattens hierarchical structures, encourages open communication, and promotes an inclusive atmosphere, fostering better team dynamics and driving enhanced results.

10.2. Implementing Meditative Practices in Leadership

Incorporating meditative practices into leadership roles doesn't necessarily entail holding team meditations or converting office spaces into calm sanctuaries. Instead, it's about transforming the way leaders approach their roles and the decisions they make.

The first step towards Meditative Leadership is incorporating mindfulness practices into your daily routine. Mindfulness is about focusing one's awareness on the present moment, calmly acknowledging and accepting one's feelings, thoughts, and bodily sensations.

☐ Start by setting aside a few minutes each day for mindfulness meditation. This can be as simple as focusing on your breath or following a guided meditation.

☐ Begin to incorporate mindfulness into everyday actions, such as walking or eating. Learning to concentrate your mind on simple actions can help enhance your focus, offering increased clarity in more complex tasks and decisions.

☐ Practice mindful listening in your interactions with team members. Rather than formulating responses or allowing your mind to wander during conversations, strive to focus squarely on what the other person is saying.

With practice, you'll start noticing changes in how you relate to your experiences, and consequently, in how you lead.

10.3. The Impact of Meditative Leadership

The adoption of Meditative Leadership carries profound benefits for both leaders and their teams. By leading from a place of mindfulness, leaders become more adaptable to change, more resilient, compassionate, and ultimately, more effective.

 Enhanced Decision-Making: Meditative Leadership calls for being fully present, which means less distraction and increased clarity. This leads to better-quality decisions, accurate judgments, and more effective problem-solving.

 Improved Communication: Meditative leaders are good listeners. Mindful listening can foster a spirit of open, honest communication, improving relationships between leaders and their teams.

 Greater Adaptability: Being able to calmly introspect allows meditative leaders to be more adaptable. They're able to objectively evaluate scenarios and make course corrections as necessary, without getting swept up in the tumult of change.

 Increased Emotional Intelligence: Meditation improves self-awareness and emotional regulation—two critical components of emotional intelligence, which is increasingly recognized as a key determinant of effective leadership.

10.4. Cultivating a Mindful Workplace

While Meditative Leadership starts with the individual, its ultimate goal is to propagate mindfulness throughout the organization, effecting a cultural shift towards a more focused and compassionate corporate environment.

☐ **Promoting Mindfulness Training:** Consider providing mindfulness training programs for employees. Provide resources for mindfulness practices and occasionally arrange group mindfulness sessions.

☐ **Encouraging Work-Life Balance:** A key element of mindfulness is compassionate self-care. Encourage balance by setting realistic expectations, reducing overtime, and promoting a healthy work-life balance.

☐ **Revising Performance Metrics:** Integrate mindfulness into performance metrics. Recognize and reward mindful behaviors, such as thoughtful decision-making, empathy, and effective communication.

By fostering a culture of mindfulness, organizations can inspire employees to fully engage with their roles, lead with more focus and clarity, and drive superior performance.

In conclusion, Meditative Leadership, inspired by the ancient wisdom of Buddhism, offers a fresh, effective approach to modern business strategy. It provides a gateway to a simultaneous transformation of both the individual and the organization, leading businesses on a path to sustainable success. Grasping at this unconventional tool may seem daunting initially, yet those who take the daring step forward will invariably experience a profound shift in their leadership style and business outcomes. Perhaps it's time for us to step back from the relentless pace of the modern corporate world and explore a fresh, mindful approach to leadership.

Chapter 11. Ethical Business, better Business: The Power of Right Action

Moral and ethical considerations have always remained integral to Buddhist teachings. Maintaining integrity and honesty isn't merely about adherence to a rigid moral code. Instead, it involves viewing these attributes as the bedrock of social and financial prosperity.

11.1. The Buddhist Concept: Right Action

Within the Buddhist Eightfold Path, Right Action (Sammā kammanta) forms the fulcrum of ethical behavior. This focuses on acting in ways that promote harmony and reduce harm. It dictates three major ways of right conduct: refrain from harming living beings, stealing, and sexual misconduct. For businesses, this can be interpreted as non-exploitation, integrity, and respect.

Modern businesses often grapple with the challenging balance between profitability and ethics. Company leaders may face quandaries where financial performance appears to conflict with ethical decision-making. However, the lens of Right Action renders these choices far less paradoxical, instead presenting a symbiotic possibility between the two considerations.

11.2. Ethical Business is Profitable Business

In the realm of business, ethical conduct can yield important advantages. For instance, companies showing a commitment to ethical business practices often witness increased brand trust and loyalty from customers. These consumers appreciate and echo their values, which in turn increases sales and profitability.

Similarly, investors too are shifting focus towards ethically run organizations. Research indicates businesses practicing good corporate governance and social responsibility yield better returns. Therefore, the argument that an ethically run organization can also be highly profitable is now increasingly anticipated and respected.

11.3. Prudent Decision-Making Fosters Resilience

Decision-making that does not objectively consider the broader implications threatens business longevity. Poor ethical behavior can cause reputational damage and legal issues that not only devastate profits but also shatter the business's long-term viability.

Meanwhile, a commitment to ethics protects the organization. It fosters a resilient culture that, while adaptive to change, remains constraint within the boundary of ethics. This ensures that a business, irrespective of market fluctuations and dire circumstances, doesn't lose its essence.

11.4. Building Trust as a Path to Success

Trust serves as the foundation for any relationship, and business is no exception. When a business shows commitment to ethical practices, it invariably builds trust with its customers, employees, partners, and the communities in which it operates. This faith fosters mutual growth, collaboration, and long-term business success.

11.5. A Holistic Approach to Employee Well-being

Right Action is also pertinent when considering the treatment of employees. Workplaces that invest efforts in corporate conduct designed to treat employees fairly and respectfully showcase less turnover and higher levels of job satisfaction among staff. This not only results in increased productivity but also bolsters the company's reputation as an employer of choice.

11.6. Compassionate Capitalism: A Win-Win Proposition

The age-old wisdom of Buddhism brings to the business table a concept of Compassionate Capitalism. This concept aligns profitability with compassion, thereby forging a path that is enriching on myriad levels.

Businesses should strive to become not just economic entities existing purely for profit, but also inclusive organizations that contribute positively to society. When businesses embrace such a compassionate approach, they find a balance between returns and social responsibility, creating a fruitful synergy that leads to sustainable and meaningful growth.

The teachings of Buddha, exemplified by the principle of Right Action, invite us to journey beyond the rigid confines of profit and loss, shareholders and stakeholders, to an entirely novel realm where ethical business is better business. A world where organization's decisions flow from a source of compassion and integrity, thereby creating an environment teeming with trust, resilience, and success. As we harness and internalize these ancient principles, we equip our businesses with tools not merely to survive but thrive in this complex corporate landscape. This is the essence of Right Action in businesses

- a powerful catalyst that propels us towards a promising and sustainable future.

www.ingramcontent.com/pod-product-compliance
Lightning Source LLC
Chambersburg PA
CBHW062305290526
45794CB00006B/2706